Library of
Davidson College

# Worldwatch Paper 80

## Planning the Global Family

Jodi L. Jacobson

December 1987

Worldwatch Institute is an independent, nonprofit research organization created to analyze and to focus attention on global problems. Directed by Lester R. Brown, Worldwatch is funded by private foundations and United Nations organizations. Worldwatch papers are written for a worldwide audience of decision makers, scholars, and the general public.

# Planning the Global Family

Jodi L. Jacobson

**Worldwatch Paper 80**
December 1987

Financial support for this paper was provided by the United Nations Fund for Population Activities. Sections of this paper may be reproduced in magazines and newspapers with acknowledgment to Worldwatch Institute.

The views expressed in this paper are those of the authors and do not necessarily represent those of Worldwatch Institute and its directiors, officers, or staff, or of funding organizations.

©Copyright Worldwatch Institute, 1987
Library of Congress Catalog Card Number 87-51447
ISBN 0-916468-81-X

**Printed on recycled paper**

# Table of Contents

| | |
|---|---|
| Introduction | 5 |
| Fertility Trends Worldwide | 7 |
| The Role of Family Planning | 11 |
| Family Planning and Health | 19 |
| Changing Contraceptive Technologies | 25 |
| The Ingredients of Success | 36 |
| Filling the Gap | 45 |
| Notes | 49 |

# Introduction

Thirty-three-year-old Socorro Cisneros de Rosales, a Central American mother of 13 children, is neither a demographer nor an economist. But in describing her own plight and that of the region as "an overproduction of children and a lack of food and work," Mrs. Cisneros speaks authoritatively on the conflict between high birthrates and declining economies that faces many in the Third World.[1]

Over the past two decades, steadily declining birthrates have contributed to significant improvements in the health and well-being of millions of people and to the growth of national economies. To date, however, only a few countries have reduced fertility rates enough to make these gains universal or to ensure that their populations will stabilize in the foreseeable future. Countries that remain on a high fertility path will find that meeting basic subsistence needs will be increasingly difficult in the years to come.

Despite lower fertility levels for the world as a whole, population increased by 86 million people in 1987, the largest annual increment ever. And declining death rates have balanced out the modest reductions in fertility of the past few years.[2] Furthermore, slower economic growth in developing countries plagued by debt, dwindling exports, and environmental degradation, means that governments can no longer rely on socioeconomic gains to help reduce births. This uncertain economic outlook raises important questions. Can governments successfully encourage fertility reductions in the face of extensive poverty? What mix of policies is most likely to promote smaller families, thereby reducing fertility and raising living standards?

Encouraging small families requires a two-pronged strategy of family planning and social change. Few countries, however, have put family planning and reproductive health care at the top of their agendas. In most industrial nations, widely available contraceptive technologies enable couples to choose the number and spacing of their children. But contraceptive methods remain unavailable or inaccessible to the

---

I am grateful to Mary Barberis, Carl Haub, Judith Jacobsen, Thomas Merrick, Jyoti Singh, and Joseph Speidel for reviewing early versions of this manuscript and for their help in gathering information. I would also like to thank Susan Norris for production assistance.

majority of women in many Third World countries. Surveys confirm that half the 463 million married women of reproductive age in Third World countries outside of China want no more children. Millions more would like to delay their next pregnancy. Meanwhile, the number of women in their childbearing years is increasing rapidly.[3]

With few exceptions, governments have not changed policies or invested in programs sufficiently to weaken the social conditions underlying high fertility. These conditions include, most significantly, the low status of women, and the high illiteracy, low wages, and ill health that customarily accompany it. Until societal attitudes change, national fertility rates are unlikely to decline significantly.

Family planning programs are essential to the success of development policies for two reasons. One, governments confronted with large and rapidly expanding populations can promote family planning to establish a balance between numbers of people and available resources. Two, where infant and maternal death rates are high due to uncontrolled fertility, family planning is essential to improving health. But most fundamental is the issue of basic human rights: In accord with the declaration signed at the 1984 International Conference on Population in Mexico City, most governments reaffirmed that the freedom to plan the number and spacing of births is a basic human right of all individuals.

Unfortunately, international support for family planning has weakened considerably in recent years. By the time the world's population surpassed 5 billion in 1987, the United States had abdicated its role as a leading supporter of reproductive rights worldwide. Political and societal disputes have converged with fiscal constraints to force legislators to cut funding for contraceptive research and both domestic and international family planning. This policy change has set worldwide family planning back by several years, dimming hopes of achieving global population stabilization by the end of next century.

Reducing birthrates to speed the development process is a goal that deserves the immediate attention of the world community one that will benefit every segment of society. For women, bearing fewer children means better health for themselves and their offspring. For

> "A country that has achieved replacement-level fertility is well on the road to a stable population size."

countries, reducing average family size increases per capita investments and alleviates pressures on the natural resources that underpin national economies. For the world, slower population growth enhances the prospects for widespread security and prosperity.

## Fertility Trends Worldwide

Childbearing trends are most clearly represented by total fertility rates, defined as the average number of children a woman will bear at prevailing levels of fertility. A country that has achieved replacement-level fertility of about 2.1 births per woman is well on the road to a stable population size. Once this level has been reached, births and deaths eventually balance out. A population at or below replacement level may continue to grow for two or three generations, however, if the group reaching childbearing age is larger than that reaching old age and dying.

With few exceptions, total fertility rates in the industrial world are at or below replacement level. In France, the United Kingdom, and the United States, for example, the rate is 1.8 births per woman; in Denmark, Italy, and West Germany, it is below 1.5. As a result of low birthrates and populations distributed about evenly among age groups, these countries will stop growing in the near future. The United Kingdom, for example, is projected to stabilize at 59 million people, about 5 percent above its current population.[4]

Developing countries can be divided into two groups. In the first, fertility rates declined significantly over the past two decades, although few have reached replacement level. In the second group, mostly countries in sub-Saharan Africa, fertility rates have not declined at all.

Twenty countries for which there are reliable data show fertility declines of more than 20 percent since 1960. (See Table 1.) The most dramatic changes took place in East Asia and Cuba, where fertility levels dropped by as much as 75 percent. Only one Middle Eastern country (Turkey) and two African countries (Egypt and Tunisia) have

Table 1: Fertility Declines in Selected Countries, 1960-87

| Country | Total Fertility Rates 1960 | 1987 | Change |
|---|---|---|---|
| | (average number of children per woman) | | (percent) |
| Singapore | 6.3 | 1.6 | −75 |
| Taiwan | 6.5 | 1.8 | −72 |
| South Korea | 6.0 | 2.1 | −65 |
| Cuba | 4.7 | 1.8 | −62 |
| China | 5.5 | 2.4 | −56 |
| Chile | 5.3 | 2.4 | −55 |
| Colombia | 6.8 | 3.1 | −54 |
| Costa Rica | 7.4 | 3.5 | −53 |
| Thailand | 6.6 | 3.5 | −47 |
| Mexico | 7.2 | 4.0 | −44 |
| Brazil | 6.2 | 3.5 | −44 |
| Malaysia | 6.9 | 3.9 | −43 |
| Indonesia | 5.6 | 3.3 | −41 |
| Turkey | 6.8 | 4.0 | −41 |
| Tunisia | 7.3 | 4.5 | −38 |
| Sri Lanka | 5.9 | 3.7 | −37 |
| India | 6.2 | 4.3 | −31 |
| Philippines | 6.6 | 4.7 | −29 |
| Peru | 6.6 | 4.8 | −27 |
| Egypt | 6.7 | 5.3 | −21 |

Source: 1960 data from Ansley Coale, "Recent Trends in Fertility in Less Developed Countries," *Science*, August 26, 1983; 1987 data from Population Reference Bureau, 1987 *World Population Data Sheet* (Washington, D.C.: 1987).

experienced fertility declines of more than a fifth since 1960. China reduced fertility rates by 56 percent since the sixties; Chile, Colombia, and Costa Rica, by more than 50 percent each. Significant reductions were also achieved in Brazil, Indonesia, Mexico, and Thailand. Nevertheless, fertility rates remain moderately high, above 3.5 children per woman, in several of these countries.

Despite some impressive gains, only four of the 20 countries listed in Table 1 achieved replacement-level fertility: Cuba, Singapore, South Korea, and Taiwan. These four have also made tremendous economic strides. In demographic terms, however, they are responsible for only a minuscule fraction of annual increases to the global population.

Trends in the more populous countries are much more important to global population growth. Between 1987 and 2007, five countries in Table 1—Brazil, China, India, Indonesia, and Mexico—will account for 37 percent of total world population growth. Cumulatively, these five will add nearly 700 million people, slightly fewer than India's current population. By 2020, India will rival China as the world's largest nation, with about 1.3 billion people. And Mexicans will then number 138 million, more people than are in all of Central America and the Caribbean today. China, with a current fertility rate of 2.4 births per woman, is the only one of these demographic giants likely to achieve replacement-level fertility in the near future.[5]

Varying fertility declines reflect economic and cultural influences on birthrates and the strength of family planning programs. Singapore, South Korea, and Taiwan have undergone rapid industrialization over the past 15 years and the ensuing economic gains reduced the desire for large families. More significantly, though, these countries were among the first to establish family planning programs. In Singapore, for example, contraceptive supplies have been widely available since the forties. In other countries, such as Brazil and India, the distribution of economic gains has been uneven. And the introduction of widespread family planning services has been relatively recent. Large differences in fertility levels exist between urban and rural areas and between various ethnic groups.

Fertility is declining much more slowly now, and in some countries appears to have reached a plateau. A recent report from the Indian National Academy of Science shows that the total fertility rate there declined by about 16 percent between 1972 and 1978, from 5.6 births per woman of reproductive age to 4.7. But the pace has slowed markedly since then. In 1987, Indian women bore on average 4.3 children, only 8 percent below the figure in 1978. Egypt and the Philippines show similar trends.[6]

Pockets of extremely high fertility—above six children per woman—still exist throughout Africa and the Middle East. (See Table 2.) Sub-Saharan Africa faces the highest fertility rates and population growth rates in the world. Nigerian women, for instance, bear nearly seven children on average. Most Middle Eastern countries also maintain high fertility levels, as do Bangladesh and Pakistan.

Table 2: Countries with High Fertility, 1987

| Country | Total Fertility Rate (average number of children per woman) | Population Growth Rate (percent) |
|---|---|---|
| Kenya | 8.0 | 3.9 |
| Afghanistan | 7.6 | 2.6 |
| Jordan | 7.4 | 3.7 |
| Tanzania | 7.1 | 3.5 |
| Zambia | 7.0 | 3.5 |
| Saudi Arabia | 6.9 | 3.1 |
| Ethiopia | 6.7 | 2.3 |
| Senegal | 6.7 | 2.8 |
| Nigeria | 6.6 | 2.8 |
| Pakistan | 6.6 | 2.9 |
| Sudan | 6.5 | 2.8 |
| Zimbabwe | 6.5 | 3.5 |
| Iran | 6.3 | 3.2 |
| Bangladesh | 6.2 | 2.7 |
| Zaire | 6.1 | 3.1 |

**Source:** Population Reference Bureau, 1987 *World Population Data Sheet* (Washington, D.C.: 1987).

A tradition of large families in countries where young people are predominant means these countries will experience massive population increases over the next generation. Pakistan's population will more than double over the next 30 years, from 105 million to well over 240 million; Nigeria's will reach 274 million, up from its current population of 109 million; and Bangladesh's 104 million will grow to 200 million.[7]

Lowering birthrates will help ease the transition from persistent poverty to sustainable development by reducing pressure on national resources. For example, a 1985 analysis by Kenya's National Council for Population and Development projected the country's future population size under two scenarios. It showed that at current fertility rates, Kenyans—now 22 million—would number 57 million in 2010, as opposed to 38 million if total fertility dropped by half to 4 children per woman. With the smaller population size, corn requirements would be reduced by 3.2 million tons, twice the amount Kenyan farmers produced in 1980.[8]

Tremendous strides have been made in the drive to reduce fertility and improve living standards over the last generation. But for too many countries, this task is not complete. By promoting smaller families, governments can ensure a better and more productive life for today's citizens and for the children yet to come.

**The Role of Family Planning**

Family planning has played an integral role in reducing fertility throughout the world. Countries such as China, Mexico, and Thailand have devoted extensive government resources to expanding services and supplying contraceptives. In Brazil, the efforts of private voluntary organizations have been key to declining birthrates. Nevertheless, in a substantial number of high fertility countries, family planning programs are weak or nonexistent, largely because governments have been slow to allocate the necessary resources. The question is: What role can family planning play to promote smaller families in low-income countries? And how can lower fertility, in turn, contribute to the development process? The recent experiences of several nations suggest a close relationship between effective voluntary family planning programs, rising levels of contraceptive use, and declining fertility, even in the absence of broad-based economic gains.

Fertility rates are most directly affected by changes in four variables: age at marriage, contraceptive use, induced abortion, and duration of breastfeeding—known in demographic parlance as the "proximate determinants" of fertility. These determinants vary in importance among societies and within a society over time depending on socioeconomic trends and government policy. Changing levels of income and education, for example, reduce fertility rates by influencing marriage patterns, desired family size, and demand for family planning.

Family planning programs primarily affect fertility by raising contraceptive prevalence—the share of married women of reproductive age who use modern contraception to prevent pregnancy. Modern birth control methods like the pill and intrauterine device (IUD) are far more effective at preventing pregnancy than their traditional counterparts, such as withdrawal. The cost and availability of birth control dictates the difference between the number of children a couple wants and the number they actually have.

Significantly, the demand for contraceptive information and supplies is rising among groups traditionally resistant to family planning, namely the urban and rural poor. Access to radio and television has had dramatic impact on the desires and aspirations of millions of people. The rapid growth of cities in developing countries, together with better transportation, mean that changing values spread more quickly throughout a country.

Most important, large families no longer offer the promise of economic security where mounting resource scarcity hinders economic development. The cycle of poverty, environmental decline, and hunger in which nearly a billion Third World people live today has contributed to the change in desired family size now evident among groups at every income and educational level.

*"Large families no longer offer the promise of economic security where mounting resource scarcity hinders economic development."*

"Unmet need," defined as the gap between the number of women who express a desire to limit fertility and the number who actually are able to do so, exists to varying degrees in virtually every developing country. This gap results from inadequate access to or knowledge of family planning methods, even where programs already exist. According to data from the World Fertility Survey (an international reproductive trends survey sponsored by the United Nations between 1974 and 1984), 40 to 50 percent of women of reproductive age in 18 developing countries desire no more children but have no access to family planning. Fertility rates could be reduced by 30 percent in these countries if unwanted births were prevented.[9]

In India, half the couples contacted in the 1980 All-India Family Planning Survey wished to limit family size, but only 28 percent were using a modern method of birth control. (See Table 3.) The gap between desired and actual family size spotlights the inadequacy of family planning programs. Two-thirds of the couples surveyed felt three children was ideal, although most couples in India have four or more. Similarly, a 1985 survey showed that while 56 percent of Egyptian women wanted no more children, only 30 percent were using contraceptives. These surveys actually define a minimum level of unmet need: Because a significant share of respondents have never even heard of a family planning method, they are unlikely to identify a need for one even if they desire smaller families.

Not surprisingly, the countries with the strongest commitment to family planning are making the greatest strides in reducing fertility, regardless of their level of development. In Indonesia, a predominantly rural country with a per capita income of $530, a well-organized national family planning program has been in operation since 1969. A 1987 government survey indicates that between 1980 and 1985 contraceptive prevalence increased from 27 to nearly 41 percent of married women of reproductive age. A striking 42 percent decline in the number of births per woman of reproductive age occurred between 1970 and 1985, with the most significant drop after 1980. Due to the government's efforts to make family planning universally available, over 80 percent of Indonesian contraceptive users rely on modern methods[10].

Table 3: Unmet Need for Family Planning in Egypt, India, Peru, and Rural Ghana

| Country | Share of Women of Reproductive Age Wanting No More Children | Using Contraception | Unmet Need |
|---|---|---|---|
| | (percent) | | |
| India | 50 | 28 | 22 |
| Egypt | 56 | 30 | 26 |
| Peru | 70 | 25 | 45 |
| Ghana Rural Areas Near Accra | 90 | 10 | 80 |

Source: "Contraceptive Use Climbs in India But Reversible Methods Are Misunderstood, Remain Little Used," *International Family Planning Perspectives*, March 1986; Hussein A.A.H. Sayed, M. Nabil El-Khorazaty, Ann A. Way, *Fertility and Family Planning in Egypt 1984* (Columbia, Md.: Egypt National Population Council and Westinghouse Public Applied Systems, 1985); "Despite Peru's Strong Population Policies, Fertility, Infant Mortality Are High, Especially in Rural Areas," *International Family Planning Perspectives*, September 1984; Robert M. Press, "Family Planning Gains Some Favor in Africa," *Christian Science Monitor*, January 7, 1983.

Examining data from the World Fertility Survey, University of Michigan sociologist Ronald Freedman showed that contraceptive use varies little among Indonesians in different social and economic groups. Couples with low living standards are almost as likely to use contraception as those with the highest standards. Professional and clerical workers are only slightly ahead of farmers with small landholdings. And villages without modern amenities like electricity have contraceptive prevalence levels about as high as those with such facilities.[11]

In Bangladesh, a deteriorating agrarian economy has raised the ante on large families just when a growing family planning program is making birth control cheaper. Agricultural wages today are below those of 150 years ago in constant dollars. Demographer Samuel Preston notes that much of the decline in real wages occurred since the fifties, a period of rapid population growth. The number of landless families has mushroomed. Parents do not see a very bright future for their children: Land scarcity has undermined traditional inheritance practices, while rising educational costs have foreclosed employment options outside the agricultural sector.[12]

Substantial unmet demand for family planning exists in Bangladesh. One study based on data from three government surveys found that the adoption of family planning methods has accelerated gradually in recent years in response to greatly improved services. Between 1969 and 1983, the share of married women who did not want additional children increased slightly, from 52 to 57 percent. Over the same period, contraceptive use increased steadily among both rural and urban women of all educational levels and all family sizes. In 1969, fully 93 percent of Bangladeshi women who wished to end childbearing were not using contraceptives; by 1983, this unmet need had declined to 71 percent, albeit still a high level. The study concludes that deteriorating economic and environmental conditions "may have influenced couples...to believe that large families are burdensome."[13]

A second study, this one carried out by the International Centre for Diarrhoeal Disease Research in the rural Matlab region of Bangladesh, compares trends in contraceptive practice between two groups of villagers from 1977 to 1984. The first group was served only by the government's family planning program. In the second group, a more extensive program was set up which included medical assistance and a broader choice of contraceptive methods. By 1984, contraceptive use within the experimental area increased to 40 percent of all married women of reproductive age, a level more than twice the control group and nearly twice that for the country as a whole. The share of women in the experimental area desiring no more children rose from 43 to 55 percent, indicating that the small-family concept was gaining ground. These changes occurred among women of all educational levels and family sizes, with the largest shifts among uneducated women.[14]

Success is rarely unequivocal. After nearly a decade of exposure to the family planning program, half the women in the Matlab Thana study who wanted to end childbearing were still not using contraception for reasons as yet unclear to the study's authors. Moreover, the most successful efforts to date in Bangladesh have been small-scale, private initiatives. Compared to other government-sponsored programs, the official Bangladeshi program is relatively weak and ineffective. Yet the studies show that a more concerted effort would pay off handsomely in Bangladesh.

The lowest contraceptive prevalence (and the highest fertility rates) are found in sub-Saharan Africa, where the use of modern methods of birth control is rising quite slowly. Until recently, most African governments firmly opposed family planning programs on the grounds that curtailing population growth would limit the region's ability to recognize its economic potential. The low status of women has made childbearing the only rite of passage for girls. And lack of funds and poor service delivery systems hinder the dissemination of information and methods outside major urban areas. Surveys show that only a fifth of Nigerian women have ever heard of a modern method of birth control. In Kenya, less than 40 percent of women familiar with at least one modern contraceptive method knew of a supply source; fewer than half of these women could reach the source on a 30-minute walk.[15]

Despite these constraints, the desire both to space and limit births is increasingly evident in some African countries, particularly among educated women and those living in urban areas. (See Figure 1.) About 37 percent of Kenyan women would like to delay their next birth and an almost equal proportion want no more children. Fifty-one percent of women in Zimbabwe and 39 percent of women in Senegal would like to delay their next birth. Governments that respond to this unmet need for family planning could have a significant impact on fertility.[16]

Evidence of fertility decline due to strong family planning programs exists in sub-Saharan Africa. In 1982, a government survey showed that contraceptive prevalence in Zimbabwe stood at 14 percent for both modern and traditional methods. That year, President Robert Mugabe committed his government to a strong family planning effort to slow population growth and promote economic development. The program was immediately incorporated into the Ministry of Health, linking it with training and outreach for maternal and child health

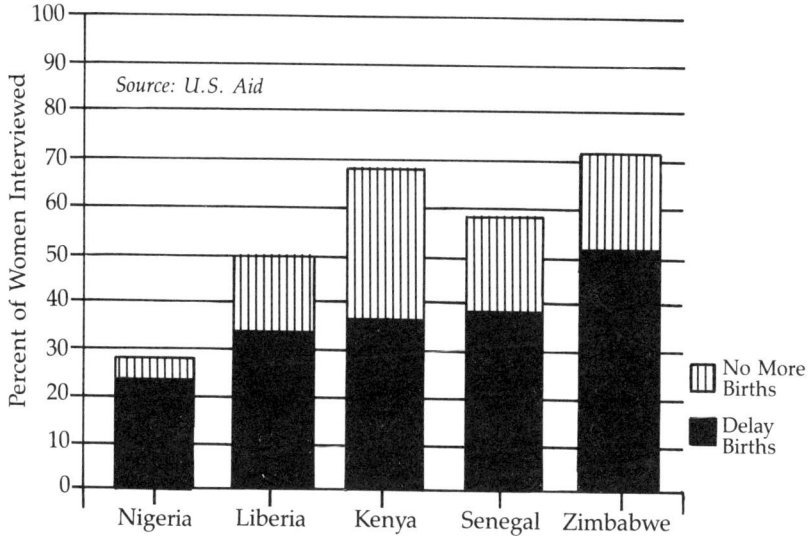

Figure 1: Demand for Family Planning in Africa, Selected Countries, 1987

care. Zimbabwe made a financial commitment unparalleled among sub-Saharan nations, allocating $24 million to the program. By 1984, total contraceptive prevalence reached 38 percent (27 percent for modern methods), a remarkable increase for any country.[17]

In Zimbabwe, fertility rates remain high despite rising contraceptive prevalence levels because most new contraceptive users want to space rather than limit their offspring. As a consequence, national reductions in fertility levels will be delayed. And high failure rates among first-time users of modern methods suggest a need for better and more extended contact between health care professionals and contraceptive users. Rather than signaling failure, these issues bring to light the need to study how programs can best respond to different circumstances.

Cultural practices that naturally limit fertility may offer an opening for new programs. In sub-Saharan Africa, the tradition of breastfeeding, which inhibits ovulation, promotes birthspacing and ensures that the untimely arrival of one infant does not interrupt the nursing pattern of the one preceding it. A 1982 study in the rural Sine-Saloum region of Senegal found that only 3 percent of women were using any contraceptive method. In the absence of breastfeeding, total fertility would nearly double from 6.4 to an estimated 12.2 births per woman.[18]

Modernization is associated with an erosion of this tradition and a corresponding increase in fertility. By promoting breastfeeding and contraceptive use simultaneously, family planning programs can help avert the rise in birthrates that often occurs during the transition from high to low fertility. Such initiatives can set the stage for later, more widespread reductions in fertility rates.

By reducing fertility levels, and hence the social expenditures necessary just to maintain the economic status quo, family planning programs can help to raise living standards. Between 1972 and 1984, for example, every peso spent on family planning by Mexico's urban social security system (IMSS) saved nine pesos that would otherwise have been spent on maternal and infant health care services. During this time, IMSS spent 38 billion pesos ($252 million) to provide nearly 800,000 women with contraceptive supplies, thus averting 3.6 million births and 363,000 abortions. Net savings for IMSS equaled 318 billion pesos ($2 billion), which was rechanneled into pension payments and expansion of general health care services.[19]

Similarly, a cost-benefit analysis of Thailand's program compared government expenditures for family planning with revenues saved as a result of births averted. The study found that increased contraceptive use prevented 2.4 million births between 1972 and 1980. Over this same period, the government saved an average of $7 for each $1 invested in family planning. Moreover, when potential benefits and costs through 2010 are calculated, the savings on each dollar increases to $16. In effect, the Thai government will have $1 billion extra to invest in social services over the next two decades.[20]

> "Encouraging fewer and safer births among women in developing countries will reduce unacceptably high rates of maternal mortality from complications of childbirth and abortion."

Family planning is not a substitute for investments in education or efforts to raise per capita incomes. But reducing fertility is integral to any economic development strategy, allowing governments to raise per capita investments in health, education, and other social services. The growing desire for smaller families shows that family planning has a major role to play in virtually every nation. Developing countries that encourage family planning may be the first to experience rapid and widespread social and economic advances.

## Family Planning and Health

Family planning is among the most basic of preventive health care strategies, though it is rarely recognized as such. Encouraging fewer and safer births among women in developing countries will reduce unacceptably high rates of maternal mortality from complications of childbirth and abortion. Moreover, by distributing condoms and increasing the public's understanding of reproductive health issues, family planning programs can help control the spread of acquired immunodeficiency syndrome (AIDS), a major threat to Third World health and economic survival.

Each year, at least a half million women worldwide die from pregnancy-related causes. Fully 99 percent of these deaths occur in the Third World, where complications arising from pregnancy and illegal abortions are the leading killers of women in their twenties and thirties. World Health Organization (WHO) officials caution that maternal deaths—those resulting directly or indirectly from pregnancy within 42 days of childbirth, induced abortion, or miscarriage—are probably twice the estimated figures. What is more, for every woman who dies, many more suffer serious, often long-term, health problems.[21]

Maternal mortality is a long-neglected, pernicious phenomenon reflecting the low status of women in many Third World societies. Poor health conditions, frequent pregnancies, and lack of access to proper medical care make childbearing dangerous. That bearing life brings death to so many women is a distressing irony. It is even more distressing given that family planning and preventive medicine could substantially reduce these losses.

Little attention has been paid to the problems of maternity relative to other health care issues, such as infant and child mortality. About half the world's countries report maternal mortality statistics to WHO. Those countries for which there are no data are all in the Third World. Although 50 of the 52 African nations collect data on infant mortality, only five have ever reported maternal mortality figures, and most of these have not been updated since 1979.[22]

In the Third World, maternal mortality accounts for some 25 percent of deaths of women aged 15 to 49. More than 3,000 maternal deaths per 100,000 live births occur annually in parts of Ethiopia and Bangladesh. (See Table 4.) By contrast, the figures in the United States and Norway are only 10 and 2, respectively. Each year, over 20,000 women die from pregnancy or related complications in Bangladesh, compared with about 500 women in the United States, a country with more than twice as many people.[23]

Illegal abortion is one of the major direct causes of maternal death. Rough estimates indicate that only half the 54 million abortions carried out annually around the world are legal. Most illegal abortions are performed under unsanitary conditions by unskilled attendants, leaving women vulnerable to serious complications and infection. By contrast, modern abortion procedures, performed under proper medical supervision in countries where they are legal, cause fewer maternal deaths than pregnancy and oral contraceptives together.[24]

Forty-four percent of women in the developing world (outside of China) live in countries where abortion is allowed only to save the mother's life. Another 10 percent live in countries where abortion is totally prohibited. Sadly, millions of women unable to obtain a legal abortion on the basis of life-threatening circumstances have subsequently died from the complications of an illegal abortion. Those who advocate restrictive abortion policies rarely acknowledge this toll on women's lives.[25]

Table 4: Maternal Mortality Ratios, Selected Countries, 1987

| Country | Maternal Mortality Ratios (deaths per 100,000 live births) | Region and Year |
|---|---|---|
| Ethiopia | 3,500[1] | Urban, 1984 |
| Bangladesh | 3,000[2] | National, 1983 |
| Senegal | 700[1] | Rural, 1983 |
| India | 400-500[2] | National, 1984 |
| Egypt | 190 | Rural, 1981-83 |
| Romania | 175 | National, 1982 |
| Mexico | 103 | National, 1978 |
| Thailand | 81 | National, 1981 |
| Chile | 73 | National, 1980 |
| United States | 10 | National, 1979 |
| Norway | 2 | National, 1981 |

[1]Unknown whether deaths from abortions included.
[2]Deaths from abortions not included.

**Source:** World Health Organization, *Maternal Mortality Rates: A Tabulation of Available Information*, FHE/85.2 (Geneva: 1985).

Estimates of the annual number of deaths due to abortion complications range from 155,000 to 204,000 women worldwide. Abortion-related deaths are especially common among poor and illiterate women living in countries with strict abortion laws. In Latin America, where legal abortion is generally restricted to cases of rape or endangerment of the woman's life, up to half of maternal deaths appear to be due to illegal abortions.[26]

In Asia, where abortion laws are generally less restrictive, more than a fifth of maternal deaths are still related to terminations of pregnancy. Abortion is illegal throughout most of Africa, and has traditionally been a little-used option because of the desirability of large families. Yet studies show the number of abortion-related deaths rising on that continent. Some groups, especially young women in urban areas frustrated by the lack of family planning methods, now resort to abortion as a means of delaying births and limiting family size.[27]

Pregnancy takes a greater toll on a woman's body in regions where malnutrition and poor health are the norm. In the Third World, pregnancy is associated with a higher incidence of health-threatening infection, vitamin and mineral deficiencies, and anemia. Due to reduced immunity, common diseases such as pneumonia and influenza cause 50 to 100 percent more deaths in pregnant than in nonpregnant women.[28]

Anemia is epidemic: Two-thirds of the pregnant women in Third World countries suffer from this condition which contributes to between 40 and 50 percent of maternal deaths. Anemic women are more likely than other women to succumb to complications at childbirth, such as hemorrhaging.[29]

Three groups of women face the highest risk of pregnancy-related deaths—those at either end of their reproductive cycle, those who bear children in rapid succession, and those who have more than four children. Due to biological factors, women under 19 or over 35 are more susceptible to complications from pregnancy. Women giving birth to children spaced less than a year apart are twice as likely to die from pregnancy-related causes than those who have children two or more years apart. In Matlab Thana, Bangladesh, health workers recorded three times as many deaths among women giving birth to their eighth child as among those giving birth to their third.[30]

At least half of all maternal deaths can be averted through a combined strategy of family planning, legal abortion, and primary health care. According to researchers Beverly Winikoff and Maureen Sullivan of the Population Council, a 25- to 35-percent reduction in fertility rates resulting from more widely available family planning would also lower maternal mortality by one-fourth. Making abortions legal and safe could reduce the toll an additional 20 to 25 percent. Making all pregnancies safer through increased investments in prenatal health care and reducing the number of high-risk pregnancies would prevent another 20 to 25 percent of deaths. Winikoff and Sullivan point out that while, theoretically, this three-pronged strategy could reduce maternal mortality by three-fourths, a 50-percent decrease is a more realistic expectation, given prevailing social and political conditions in many countries.[31]

Wherever women marry early and rely on childbearing as a sign of status, family planning methods take longer to gain widespread acceptance. Early marriage is common in most developing countries. Childbearing is typically an immediate and intended outcome, resulting in a high proportion of teenage pregnancies. Thus, reducing high-risk pregnancies among young women aged 15 to 19 may be a more difficult task than among older women who have established their families. Moreover, entrenched attitudes and cultural and religious influences often make abortion laws difficult to change. And primary health care remains inadequate despite its huge potential for improving the quality of life in developing countries.

These obstacles notwithstanding, establishing integrated family planning and health strategies would be well worth the investment. Village-based paramedics and midwives could teach women the benefits of birth-spacing, breastfeeding, prenatal care, and contraceptive use. Small-scale maternity centers—on the order of one for every 4,000 people—could promote simple solutions to some of the most pervasive maternal health problems, by providing, for instance, iron supplements to treat anemia. Linked with regional facilities run by doctors, such clinics would constitute a pivotal link between rural populations and the often urban-based medical community. Assuming that maternal deaths run as high as 1 million per year, family planning and health care would save at least 500,000 women's lives annually, and improve the health of millions more.[32]

Abortion is not a preferable option to pregnancy prevention. But laws cannot suppress abortion practices; they can only make them more or less safe and costly. Although reforming restrictive abortion laws may stir opposition, failing to do so means a continued and serious loss of women's lives, and an emotional and economic drain for societies in general.

Increasing maternal survival through family planning will also improve child survival and nutrition prospects. Children whose mothers die in childbirth are less likely to receive adequate care or nourishment, increasing their health risks. Sixty to 70 percent of infants born to women who die in childbirth do not survive the neonatal period, and the risks extend to children aged one to five. The tremendous reductions in infant and child mortality to be gained from birthspacing and breastfeeding have been well documented elsewhere. In the long run, higher rates of child survival translate into lower birth rates because mothers bear fewer children to reach a desired family size.[33]

Ironically, new, rather than traditional, reproductive health threats may push family planning services to the top of national agendas. By October 1987, the total number of reported AIDS cases worldwide (of persons who already show signs of illness) had exceeded 60,000, more than one-sixth of which were in developing countries. Although the United States leads the world with nearly 42,000 documented cases as of September 1987, the potential devastation from AIDS appears to be a far greater threat in the Third World. Poverty, malnutrition, and poor health are likely contributors to the rapid spread of this deadly plague. WHO estimates that between 5 to 10 million people around the world may now be infected with the virus and at least 2 million of them are in Africa. Approximately 4,000 cases have been found in Latin America and the Caribbean. Current health care problems may only foreshadow the far more serious public health burdens to come.[34]

Transmission of this new virus through sexual contact is the single greatest route of infection. Reuse of contaminated needles and surgical instruments as well as infection of infants during pregnancy or childbirth have also been important factors in the spread of AIDS. Evidence exists that other sexually transmitted diseases common throughout the developing world, such as syphilis and gonorrhea, increase the risk of contracting the AIDS virus.[35]

AIDS prevention and education can best be carried out by family planning and related health programs. Next to total abstinence, condoms offer the best protection against the spread of sexually transmitted diseases. Yet, primarily for cultural reasons, condoms are rarely

> "AIDS prevention and education can best be carried out by family planning and related health programs."

used in most of the Third World. Excluding China, fewer than one-fifth of the world's 40 million condom users live in developing countries. Increasing the availability of condoms and linking their use with better health may slow the spread of AIDS. Instructing paramedics on the dangers of reusing needles or performing routine procedures with unsanitary implements, and securing adequate supplies of medical equipment will insure that the health-care community itself is not responsible for spreading the virus.[36]

Scientists currently believe that between 25 and 50 percent of those infected with the virus that can lead to AIDS will die in the next ten years. In developing countries, this disease will primarily afflict individuals aged 20 to 49. Both pregnancy- and AIDS-related deaths strike people in their prime, taking a tremendous toll in human life and productive capacity. The need for public education about reproductive health is greater than ever.[37]

**Changing Contraceptive Technologies**

Nearly 30 years after the introduction of oral contraceptives, millions of couples in the developing world remain without the means to plan their families. Poor supply and distribution networks are part of the problem. But contraceptive prevalence in the Third World remains low, in part, because few of the methods currently available fit the lifestyles or pocketbooks of potential users. Today's menu of technologies is not versatile enough, nor is it changing quickly enough, to meet the needs of a highly diverse and growing world population.

About 370 million of the 860 million married couples of reproductive age worldwide use modern contraceptives, a prevalence rate of 43 percent. (See Table 5.) Among couples in developing countries outside of China, use of modern methods is much lower than the world average. Although more than half indicate a desire to practice family planning, only 27 percent actually do.

At least nine reversible contraceptives are on the market, including hormonal methods which inhibit ovulation. Their distribution is highly skewed to particular regions or countries. Eighty-three million

Table 5: Estimated Use of Effective Birth Control Methods,[1] 1986

| Birth Control Method | China | Other Developing Countries | Industrial Countries | World |
|---|---|---|---|---|
| | (millions of users) | | | |
| Female Sterilization | 53 | 45 | 15 | 113 |
| IUDs | 59 | 13 | 11 | 83 |
| Oral Contraceptives | 9 | 28 | 27 | 64 |
| Condoms | 5 | 12 | 28 | 45 |
| Male Sterilization | 17 | 18 | 8 | 43 |
| Other Effective Methods[2] | 3 | 8 | 13 | 24 |
| Total Users | 146 | 124 | 102 | 372 |
| Total Couples at Risk[3] | 200 | 463 | 197 | 860 |
| | | (percent) | | |
| Contraceptive Prevalence (users as share of those at risk) | 73 | 27 | 52 | 43 |
| | | (millions) | | |
| Abortions | 12 | 16 | 26 | 54 |

[1]Effective or modern methods includes all birth control methods except natural family planning (rhythm), withdrawal, abstinence, or breastfeeding.
[2]Includes diaphragms, sponges, injectables, and implants.
[3]Total number of couples of reproductive age at risk of pregnancy. Does not include those currently pregnant or noncontraceptively sterile.

**Source:** Population Crisis Committee, "Access to Birth Control: A World Assessment," Briefing Paper No. 19, Washington, D.C., October 1987.

women have IUDs, the most prevalent reversible method; nearly three-fourths of them are in China. By contrast, the 64 million users of oral contraceptives are more evenly divided between the Third World and industrial countries. Nearly 60 million people, about two-thirds

> "Natural family planning—also known as the rhythm method or periodic abstinence—has consistently high failure rates."

of whom live in the industrial world, rely primarily on condoms, diaphragms, and sponges.

Contraceptives vary significantly in their effectiveness depending on the skill and consistency with which a given method is used. As a group, hormonal methods, including implants and injectables, are the most effective. Birth control pills—the most established hormonal method—have the widest failure range in that group. The effectiveness of these oral contraceptives, which must be taken every day, depends on a high level of individual motivation and an understanding of self-administered drugs.

In the United States, for example, oral contraceptives are 98 percent effective, meaning that for every 100 women using the pill regularly for one year, two are likely to get pregnant. A 1985 study of women in the Philippines shows a very different picture: Failure rates reached 19 per 100 due to improper use.[38]

Injectable contraceptives have been on the market for about a decade and are among the most effective hormonal methods. Approximately 6.5 million women around the world use injectables, one-sixth of whom are Chinese. The injectable Depo-Provera, approved in 90 countries, prevents conception for three months. Injectables effective over a one-month period are used primarily in China and Latin America.[39]

At the other end of the scale of effectiveness, natural family planning—also known as the rhythm method or periodic abstinence—has consistently high failure rates. Worldwide, between 10 million and 15 million people use rhythm, most of whom live in industrial countries. This technique requires a woman to time her ovulatory cycle by charting bodily functions, such as basal temperature, on a daily basis. Because a significant proportion of women everywhere experience highly variable menstrual cycles, fertile periods may be hard to calculate, and reliance on this method can often lead to unwanted pregnancy. Women without minimal education are unlikely to understand reproduction well enough to achieve even moderate levels of effectiveness with this method. Apart from other drawbacks, periodic abstinence requires a degree of cooperation between husband and wife that is unusual in many cultures.[40]

More than 60 percent of women in most industrial nations practice family planning. (See Table 6). While similar levels of contraceptive prevalence are evident among countries such as Belgium, Italy, the United Kingdom, the Netherlands, and the United States, the share of effective methods versus less effective methods varies significantly, as do the number of abortions.

In both Italy, a predominantly Catholic country, and the United Kingdom, close to three-quarters of married women of reproductive age use contraceptives. In the United Kingdom, close to half use effective methods of birth control, while in Italy less than a fifth do. As a result, Italian women experience much higher rates of contraceptive failure. Italy's low fertility rate is maintained only through a high abortion rate. In 1984, nearly twice as many abortions were performed per 100 live births in Italy as in England and Wales combined, 39 as opposed to 21.[41]

Induced abortion keeps birthrates low in most Eastern European countries where contraceptives are often officially proscribed in accord with pronatalist government policies. Like Italy, Bulgaria's high contraceptive prevalence rate is characterized by heavy reliance on less effective methods. Bulgaria's fertility rate is 2.0, an anomaly explained by the nation's abortion rate, among the highest in the world. In 1984, 92 abortions were performed per 100 live births.[42]

Contraceptive prevalence rates in China and Thailand, remarkably high for Third World countries at 74 and 65 percent respectively, approximate that of the United States. Interestingly, 22 percent of American women report using less effective methods of birth control, including barrier methods and variations on the rhythm method, compared to only 4 percent in China and 5 percent in Thailand. Theoretically, diaphragms and condoms are as effective in preventing pregnancy as are IUDs. In practice, misuse of these devices results in high recorded failure rates. Although continuous research on pills and IUDs has made them safer and more effective over the past decade, persistent misconceptions about these two contraceptives

Table 6: Contraceptive Prevalence[1], Selected Countries

| Country | Total Contraceptive Prevalence | Effective Methods | High Risk Methods |
|---|---|---|---|
| | (percent) | | |
| Belgium | 85 | 40 | 45 |
| Italy | 78 | 17 | 61 |
| United Kingdom | 77 | 52 | 25 |
| Bulgaria | 76 | 7 | 69 |
| Netherlands | 75 | 58 | 17 |
| Hungary | 74 | 47 | 27 |
| China | 74 | 70 | 4 |
| United States | 68 | 46 | 22 |
| Thailand | 65 | 60 | 5 |
| Brazil | 52 | 52 | — |
| Peru | 43 | 15 | 28 |
| Indonesia | 42 | 36 | 6 |
| Zimbabwe | 38 | 27 | 11 |
| India | 34 | 23 | 11 |
| Egypt | 25 | 22 | 3 |
| Bangladesh | 22 | 14 | 8 |
| Kenya | 17 | 9 | 8 |
| Nigeria | 5 | 1 | 4 |
| Senegal | 4 | 1 | 3 |
| Ethiopia | 2 | 2 | — |

[1]Contraceptive prevalence denotes the number of married women of reproductive age who are protected from pregnancy by contraceptives, including contraceptive sterilization. In developing countries, contraceptive prevalence includes women in consensual union; in the United States and other industrial countries, it does not.

**Source:** W. Parker Mauldin, Sheldon J. Segal, *Prevalence of Contraceptive Use In Developing Countries: A Chart Book* (New York: Rockefeller Foundation, 1986).

have caused many American women to turn to less reliable barrier methods, heightening the risk of unintended pregnancy. By contrast, government programs in China and Thailand have successfully promoted modern methods with low failure rates, such as IUDs and hormonal contraceptives. Disseminating better information on contraceptive methods will dispel myths and cut down on the number of unintended pregnancies and induced abortions that occur each year.[43]

No one contraceptive can fit the needs of every couple any more than one eyeglass prescription can correct all vision problems. In many cultures, for example, the diaphragm is considered undesirable because women are uncomfortable using this method. It may also be impractical where water for washing is in short supply. Though the pill is relatively inexpensive, it may be a highly ineffective method where primary health care is poor and contraceptive supplies uncertain. And unexpected or unpleasant side effects can cause considerable anxiety among women in countries where medical advice is hard to come by. First-year discontinuation rates between 20 and 40 percent among new pill- and IUD-users in the Third World indicate that these methods will not be effective in meeting the needs of most women in these countries.[44]

A product's safety, real and perceived, is one of the most important attributes of any contraceptive. Every method entails health risks and benefits that tend to vary with the user's age, general health, and reproductive history, representing a trade-off between convenience and safety. Oral contraceptives are associated with reduced risks of certain pelvic infections, of ovarian and uterine cancer, and of ectopic pregnancy. On the other hand, they are also coupled with increased risks of cardiovascular disease among women who smoke and those over age 35. Health risks of particular methods also change from one population to another: In the Third World, where the incidence of cardiovascular disease is relatively low, hormonal methods carry fewer risks than for women in industrial countries.[45]

Concerns about side effects and safety have surrounded Depo-Provera since its introduction. Animal studies have raised concern about links to breast and uterine cancer, although studies on humans

> "Advances in contraceptive technology that address concerns about safety and side effects will help speed the transition from high to low fertility."

remain inconclusive. As a result, Depo-Provera has not been approved in the United States.[46]

Perceived risks, such as those from unexpected side effects, can weigh heavily on an individual's choice of contraceptive method. Prolonged amenorrhea (absence of menstruation) can be particularly distressing in societies where a normal menstrual cycle signifies health or the absence of pregnancy. Menstrual irregularities are the most commonly cited reason women give for discontinued use of injectables. Contraceptive methods such as Depo-Provera which interrupt or change menstrual cycles have higher discontinuation rates than those with fewer or less-pronounced side effects. In Mexico, for example, women prefer monthly injectables over the longer-acting Depo-Provera because the return of menses reassures them of health and reminds them of the need for another injection. Advances in contraceptive technology that address concerns about safety and side effects will help speed the transition from high to low fertility around the world.[47]

Long-acting, inexpensive birth control methods are more likely to serve the needs of low-income consumers in developing countries. In this category, recently developed hormonal implants show considerable promise. One such product, NORPLANT, is the most effective reversible contraceptive yet developed, offering protection against pregnancy for five years. Small permeable rods filled with timed-release hormones are implanted under the skin of the upper arm in a simple surgical procedure. The rods can be removed at any time. NORPLANT has already been approved in 10 countries, including China, Colombia, Finland, Indonesia, Sweden, and Thailand, and is still undergoing evaluation in 26 others. A two-year implant, NORPLANT-2, is under study in several countries. The price tag for NORPLANT runs about $2.80 per year of protection, a cost that can be significantly reduced as production increases.[48]

The production schedule of a new contraceptive from laboratory to market availability may take 15 years or more under good conditions. Contraceptives evolve from a lengthy process of basic and applied research, product development, testing, marketing, and safety evaluation. In order to be registered in the United States and most other countries, experimental methods must pass muster under a series of animal and human clinical studies that usually take more than a decade to complete. Relatively few of the many leads scientists follow result in a marketable product. Not surprisingly, contraceptive development is an expensive and uncertain undertaking.[49]

Several new hormonal methods aimed at Third World consumers are in varying stages of development. WHO is investigating two new monthly injectables, Cycloprovera and HRP102, both of which will be tested in clinical trials beginning in 1988. Biodegradable injectables and implants, which break down over time and do not require surgical removal, are in the early stages of testing. All of these are more effective and have fewer side effects than their currently available counterparts. Market introduction of more revolutionary methods, like a two-year pregnancy vaccine, a reversible contraceptive for men that reduces sperm count, and chemicals for nonsurgical female sterilization, is still far off. How quickly these methods become available hinges on the amount of money and scientific effort invested in contraceptive research and development.[50]

Each new contraceptive technology results in an increase in the total number of users worldwide which in turn translates into lower fertility rates. Unfortunately, the prospects for developing and disseminating new methods are not bright. Although the largest potential for sales is now in the developing world, industrial countries—in particular the United States—remain the seat of technical know-how and financial power. In the Third World, only China, India, and Mexico have even fledgling contraceptive research and development programs.[51]

Measured in constant dollars, global funding for overall reproductive research—including basic nondirected research, contraceptive research and development, and safety evaluation—peaked in 1973. (See Figure 2.) Since then, European contributions to the field have declined in both constant and current dollars. The U.S. expenditure, averaging roughly 75 percent of the total since 1965, has declined by 23 percent in real terms since 1978. China and India alone among Third World countries have spent more than $1 million annually in

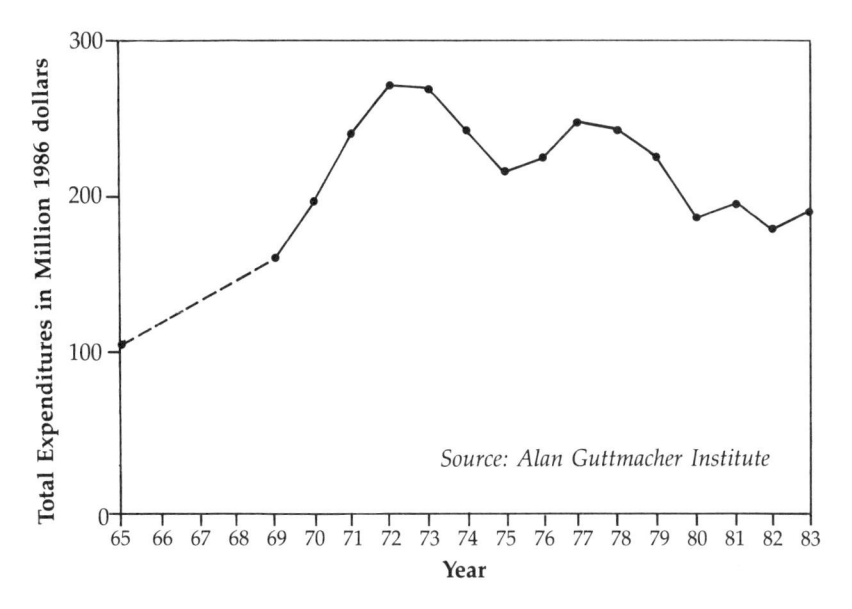

Figure 2: Worldwide Expenditures for Reproductive Research, Contraceptive R & D, and Safety Evaluation, 1965-1983

these areas. Moreover, cutbacks in public support for contraceptive research funding come at a time when the private sector is moving away from developing new methods, placing the burden of contraceptive evolution on often cash-poor nonprofit research institutions.[52]

Trends in the United States have adversely affected the contraceptive field. The development and manufacture of contraceptive products has been largely the domain of the pharmaceutical industry, with U.S. firms at the forefront. But these companies have virtually stopped producing new contraceptives for several reasons. First, U.S. Food and Drug Administration (FDA) regulations for contraceptive drugs are much stricter than those for other therapeutic agents, a policy probably holding over from the fifties when U.S. government funds could not be used to research birth control methods. These standards have raised the costs of developing and testing new products. Second, changes in patent protection laws have reduced the profits a company can expect. Third, diminishing U.S. support for population issues in general has resulted in reduced funding for the development of new technologies.

Private sector expenditures worldwide continue to focus on methods appropriate to markets in the industrial world, including new formulations of the birth control pill and postovulatory methods, such as RU 486 (the so-called French pill), which induces menstruation in the first weeks of pregnancy. Many of the newer methods involve small profit margins because they are long-acting and are tailored to low-income customers. As private industry has shied away from developing these products, eight publicly funded organizations have stepped into the void. (See Table 7.) These groups include the Contraceptive Development Branch of the Center for Population Research, part of the U.S. National Institute of Child Health and Human Development and the world's largest funder of contraceptive development; the Human Reproduction Program of the World Health Organization; and the New York-based Population Council's International Committee for Contraception Research, the developer of NORPLANT.

Controversies surrounding particular contraceptive methods have converged with a mounting U.S. insurance crisis to restrict liability coverage, thereby discouraging new product development. For example, the Dalkon Shield IUD was taken off the market by its U.S.-based producer in the early seventies after it became clear that risks of developing pelvic inflammatory disease and other serious complications were much greater for women using the shield over other IUDs. Problems with the Dalkon Shield tainted the reputations of newer and safer IUDs, such as the Copper T380A, leading manufacturers to withdraw them. By January 1987, the IUD was no longer an option for most American women. Recently, the Population Council joined forces with a small manufacturing company to put popular IUDs back on the market.[53]

Contraceptive distribution has also been colored by politics. For many years, the United States Agency for International Development (AID), the world's single largest bilateral funder of family planning activities,

Table 7. Annual Average Public and Private Expenditures for Contraceptive Product Development, 1980-83

| Method | Total Expenditures | Share from Private Sector | Share from Public Sector |
|---|---|---|---|
|  | (million dollars) | (percent) | |
| **Established Methods** | | | |
| Oral contraceptives | 6.75 | 97 | 3 |
| Barrier methods | 1.63 | 39 | 61 |
| Intrauterine Devices | 1.06 | 52 | 48 |
| Spermicides | 1.05 | 51 | 49 |
| Natural Family Planning | 0.21 | 17 | 83 |
| Condoms | 0.07 | 100 | — |
| **New Methods** | | | |
| Postovulatory | 6.89 | 81 | 19 |
| Nonsteroid Ovulation Inhibitor | 5.54 | 57 | 43 |
| Male Contraceptives | 3.65 | 35 | 65 |
| Vaccines | 2.26 | 9 | 91 |
| Implants | 1.92 | — | 100 |
| Injectables | 1.27 | 29 | 71 |
| Vaginal Rings | 0.99 | — | 100 |
| Tubal Sterilization | 0.43 | — | 100 |
| Other | 2.72 | 100 | — |
| Multiple[1] | 15.12 | — | 100 |
| Total | 51.37 | | |

[1] Grants given for research on several different methods which could not be broken down.

**Source:** Adapted from Linda Atkinson, Richard Lincoln, and Jacqueline Darroch Forrest, "The Next Contraceptive Revolution," *International Family Planning Perspectives*, December 1985.

enabled many countries to create and maintain programs by providing contraceptive supplies at cost. Because by law AID cannot distribute any contraceptive product not approved by the FDA—even in countries where the product is already approved—the decline in industry efforts to develop and license new methods has ramifications far beyond the U.S. market. The Reagan administration, in line with the demands of the religious right, has further discouraged the development of effective contraceptives and their distribution in the Third World. Programs emphasizing less effective but more politically acceptable methods, such as rhythm, have taken precedence. AID's budget for natural family planning techniques grew from $800,000 in 1981 to nearly $8 million in 1985.[54]

Reduced funding and an inhospitable political climate are delaying the development and introduction of contraceptive technology just as the demand for new methods is escalating. About $100 million is needed annually through 2000 to take new products out of the lab and put them onto the market. Creating an international consortium of public and private groups to promote cooperation on contraceptive research and recommend uniform regulatory standards among countries would speed that development process.

The number of couples of reproductive age will increase by about 600 million over the next decade. To achieve global population stabilization by the end of the next century, 65 to 70 percent of all married couples would have to be using contraception to space and limit their families. While the perfect contraceptive—absolutely safe, 100 percent effective, inexpensive, easy to distribute and to administer—may never be developed, it is within the grasp of the international community to significantly expand the range of contraceptive choice while making currently available methods safer and less expensive.[55]

## The Ingredients of Success

Without fertility declines, many governments cannot hope to make the investments necessary to improve human welfare and encourage economic development. But a number of political and social obstacles remain for countries wishing to reduce births, improve health, and raise living standards. Attaining population stabilization will depend on fundamental changes in the way governments shape population policies, the degree to which they make accessible contraceptive supplies and information, and the steps they take to improve the status of women and increase their access to education.

Governments can use a mix of policies to hasten the transition to lower fertility. Population-related policies, such as laws governing minimum age at marriage, delivery of family planning services, and the importation or manufacture of contraceptive methods, directly affect the determinants of fertility. Official sanction of family planning efforts in the form of revised policies and legal codes is likely to increase acceptance of these services and help to dispel widespread myths and misconceptions about contraception. Public policies concerning development indirectly affect fertility by influencing economic opportunities, social services, literacy, mortality and the status of women.

Over the past decade, there have been promising changes in the attitudes of African officials toward population policy and family planning. Thirteen of the 42 sub-Saharan countries have issued explicit population policies. Eleven of these countries, including Botswana, Kenya, Rwanda, Senegal, Uganda, and Zambia, have incorporated policies specifically aimed at population problems into their development plans. In discussing demographic trends, leaders have cited environmental degradation, unemployment, and the difficulty of raising living standards among their growing concerns. In the words of one Kenyan official, "If more and more people keep pouring into a country that can only deliver so much, you can expect political unrest, serious shortage of food and everything else that people need to live, and in general, chaos."[56]

Kenya became the first sub-Saharan nation to make fertility reduction a national goal when it began its family planning program 20 years ago. Policies, of course, are a necessary but not sufficient part of efforts to reduce fertility. Kenya's fertility remains high despite its early proclamations on the importance of family planning. The reluctance of some public officials to implement family planning programs, religious and tribal attitudes in favor of procreation, and the generally low status of women in Kenyan society have thwarted more substantial reductions in fertility.[57]

Most important, perhaps, is the disparity between the strength of a policy statement and the real yardstick of priorities, government expenditures. Putting money into family planning programs is what really counts. Kenya, like many other African nations, has not matched its stated commitment with financial resources. Family planning remains inaccessible to many of those who want to limit family size. According to the leader of a Rift Valley women's group, transport for the 15-mile trip to the clinic nearest her area is costly and unreliable. She notes, "If women in the Western world had to travel the distances our women in rural areas are expected to cover to meet an inefficient service, they would be discouraged as well." Greater gains will be made where rhetoric is reflected by investments. Zimbabwe's measured progress is evidence that a carefully planned and well-funded program can be implemented in a sub-Saharan nation.[58]

How programs are designed and whether or not they receive government support will determine their impact on birthrates. Any program not sensitive to the particular social and cultural constraints of a given country is doomed to failure. Early pilot programs undertaken in the fifties in Taichung, China, showed that no additional gains were made in contraceptive prevalence if the program focused on both husbands and wives. Consequently, program administrators reoriented their outreach to women only. In orthodox Muslim societies, such as are found in Pakistan and parts of Bangladesh, husbands are integral to program success. Because orthodox Muslim women often live in "purdah"—a tradition restricting them to the confines of their homes—men are the most likely recipients of contraceptive information and the subsequent supply source for their wives. Similarly, in parts of Africa, men, particularly village leaders, play a crucial role in the success of such programs.[59]

Targeting specific subgroups with an expressed desire for smaller families can help to crystallize emerging values and spread them throughout a society. By increasing access to contraceptive supplies and information, well-designed family planning programs help spread the idea that it is not only possible but acceptable for indi-

> "Any program not sensitive to the particular social and cultural constraints of a given country is doomed to failure."

viduals to plan their families and their futures. Especially in rural areas of developing countries, an individual's choices and actions are most heavily influenced by those of relatives, friends, and neighbors. The first residents in a small town or village to practice birth control and have fewer children may be the vanguard of an evolution in values. Eventually the changing mores they represent are diffused throughout society, giving legitimacy to the choice of smaller families.

Today's family planning successes—Taiwan, Thailand, Indonesia— began with a flexible, small-scale approach, positively reinforcing the trend toward fertility control. In Taiwan, for example, the number of living sons in a family was a key determinant in a couple's decision to stop having children. Efforts were directed at women with at least two living children and one son, since few women were likely to stop bearing children until they had achieved this mix of offspring. A significant share of all Taiwanese women in this group, however, wanted no more children. As a result, contraceptive prevalence rose quickly within the subgroup, providing a successful foothold for the family planning program.[60]

Realistic goals are an essential aspect of any national population policy. Programs that attempt to enforce norms—such as a two-child family—upon society before they have some cultural acceptance are usually unsuccessful. Sociologist Ronald Freedman notes that, "Setting a goal of a two child family as soon as possible may be a necessary and rational [long-term] policy goal." But, "to press for only two, when the real potential for decreasing fertility [in the short-run] is to encourage reducing desired family size from six children to four, makes the effort appear alien and ridiculous."[61]

Countries that do not start now to reduce fertility may face stark choices later, however. The conflicts between individual desires and societal goals that result from excessive population growth are evident in China's one-child family program, perhaps the best known, and most controversial, of all fertility reduction campaigns.

In 1953, the first census taken in China revealed a rapidly growing population of about 582 million. But Mao Zedong, Communist Party Chairman at that time, did not see China's expanding millions as a problem. Less than 30 years later the Chinese numbered 1 billion people, more than a fifth of the world's population living on 7 percent of the world's arable land. By the seventies, years of famine, poverty, and political upheaval had convinced China's leadership of the need for a rigorous family planning campaign.[62]

Today's one-child family program evolved out of a series of strategies that began in the early seventies with the Wan Xi Shao ("Later, Longer, Fewer") program. This strategy encouraged delayed marriage, longer birth intervals, and smaller families. Even so, China's population continued to grow rapidly. As a result, policymakers enacted the one-child family policy in order to hold the population to about 1.2 billion just after the turn of the century.[63]

The policy, intended to last through 2000, offers a series of incentives and disincentives. Substantial pay increases, better housing, longer maternity leaves, and priority access to education are among the benefits offered to one-child families. Heavy fines and social criticism await couples who bear more than one child. China's original policy, often seen as monolithic in its application, actually allows certain segments of the population to have more than one child. Urban couples are generally expected to adhere to the policy. But ethnic minorities and rural couples—80 percent of the nation's population— are allowed two or more.[64]

Surveys of both rural and urban couples indicate that ideal family size—at least among some groups—is at two or more children. In fact, between 1980 and 1984, half of new births occurred in families that already had one child. In 1987, China's birthrate rose from 18 per 1,000 population to nearly 21. A strong preference for male children is the single most important reason for this increase. Couples with one female child are eager to try again for a son, who, by tradition, remains with his parents even after he marries, helping to support them as they grow old.[65]

The success of the Chinese policy has been to mobilize people at the community level to achieve a common good, that of slowing population growth to improve the quality of life. Former U.S. Assistant Secretary of State Marshall Green writes, "The Chinese place great emphasis on the responsibility of those who are living to those who come after us." Yet by temporarily subsuming individual desires to the needs of society, the Chinese have been accused by the United States of condoning coercive abortion policies. The charges leveled at China by the Reagan administration have yet to be substantiated by any U.S. agency.[66]

Several other countries have turned to incentives in their attempts to influence fertility trends. Most such programs have targeted individuals or couples, such as programs in India and Bangladesh offering financial incentives for sterilization. Several have experienced uneven success, and in some cases have incited charges of coercion.

Government policies that bias contraceptive choice by manipulating prices, regulations, and supplies to favor one method over another often backfire. In India, for example, nearly 83 percent of contraceptive users are sterilized. During the mid-seventies, Prime Minister Indira Gandhi presided over a nationwide fertility control campaign which strongly promoted sterilization over other contraceptive methods. Evidence of coercion and forced sterilization quickly brought the campaign to a halt. While the Indian government's goal of reducing fertility levels was laudable, its tactics proved self-destructive. Public suspicion of government-sponsored programs remains so high today that acceptance of reversible methods is slow in taking hold.[67]

On the other hand, experimental incentive programs aimed at overall community participation and development have shown some promise. A pilot program carried out in northeastern Thailand tested the effects of community-level incentives on contraceptive prevalence. Loan funds of $2,000 each were set up in several villages in conjunction with a family planning and health program. Initially, loans to individuals were based on character, credit-worthiness, and the project to be carried out. After the program became established, preference was given to applicants who were practicing family planning. Members of the loan fund received shares and dividends on the basis of the contraceptive method used; more effective methods had higher values. As the level of contraceptive prevalence within a village increased, so did the total amount of the loan fund.[68]

The Thai program was designed to prevent coercion. Money was not subtracted from a loan fund if contraceptive prevalence fell; shares in the loan fund and the right to borrow were not taken away from those who chose not to continue using contraceptives. And interest rates were similar to those prevailing in the Thai government's rural credit program.

At the end of two years, loans totalling $72,000 had been granted for small-scale income-generating projects, such as pig and silk farming and cassava cultivation. During that period, contraceptive prevalence in the experimental villages rose from 46 to 75 percent; in the control villages from 51 to 57 percent. By mixing small family incentives with programs to increase community self-sufficiency, this experiment demonstrated the link between lower fertility and higher standards of living.[69]

Family planning has the most pronounced impact on fertility rates where better health and education encourage smaller families, raising demand for contraceptive information and supplies. In a 1983 study of changes in crude birthrates (the number of births per 1,000 people in a population) in 83 countries between 1960 and 1980, sociologist Phillips Cutright compared the effect on fertility levels of several social and economic indicators, including literacy rates, health, family planning efforts, levels of urbanization, and per capita income and energy use. He found that fertility levels were much more closely related to the social indicators—literacy, life expectancy, and family planning effort—than to any measure of economic development.[70]

Levels of education are among the most important determinants of fertility rates. Promoting literacy and educational achievement, particularly among women, generally increases average age at marriage, female employment, and the use of contraceptives. Later marriage reduces the total amount of time a couple has to bear children. A 1980 survey in the Indian state of Kerala, found that the average age at marriage for women with no schooling was 17, while those with nine or more years of schooling married at 22 years and over. Contraceptive use rises as women are better able to understand how to use particular methods and what side effects to expect. More importantly, changing employment and educational aspirations among women tend to reduce their dependency on husbands and male children.[71]

Interestingly, where overall educational levels are very low, fertility rates seem to rise among women with one to three years of education. (See Table 8.) This trend is seen in Bangladesh, Kenya, and the Philippines. Women with at least a primary school education respond more accurately in fertility surveys than women with no education. Moreover, children born to women with at least a basic education have higher survival rates due to better nutrition and sanitation, pushing up fertility rates in the short run. Over the long run, birthrates fall among all groups as general levels of education rises.

Table 8. Total Fertility Rate by Female Educational Level

|  | Years of Education | | | |
|---|---|---|---|---|
| Country | 0 | 1-3 | 4-6 | 7+ |
|  | (Average number of children per woman) | | | |
| Costa Rica | 5.0 | 5.0 | 3.6 | 2.7 |
| Ecuador | 7.8 | 7.2 | 5.3 | 2.7 |
| Pakistan | 6.5 | 5.4 | 6.1 | 3.1 |
| Mexico | 8.1 | 7.5 | 5.8 | 3.3 |
| Peru | 7.3 | 6.8 | 5.1 | 3.3 |
| Sudan | 6.5 | 5.6 | 5.0 | 3.4 |
| Philippines | 5.4 | 7.0 | 6.2 | 3.8 |
| Morocco | 6.4 | 5.2 | 4.4 | 4.2 |
| Bangladesh | 6.1 | 6.4 | 6.7 | 5.0 |
| Kenya | 8.3 | 9.2 | 8.4 | 7.3 |

**Source:** United Nations, Department of International Economic and Social Affairs, "Education and Fertility: Selected Findings from the World Fertility Survey Data," New York, 1986.

Women hold a paradoxical place in many societies. As mothers and wives, they often bear sole responsiblity for childrearing and domestic duties. In many cultures, they are bound by custom and necessity to contribute to household income; in some, they are the only breadwinners. Despite their role as the linchpins of society, women, particularly in the developing world, have few rights under the law regarding land tenure, marital relations, income, or social security.

In traditional African societies, women are required to be economically self-sufficient but remain legally and socially dependent on husbands and parents. Usually, African women are completely responsible for child care, cooking, cleaning, and food processing. They are responsible for at least half the effort needed to care for animals, repair homes, and market surplus products. They are almost entirely responsible for water and fuel supplies and food production, and are therefore most closely affected by ecological disruptions such as water shortages, deforestation, and loss of land productivity due to soil erosion.[72]

Subsistence agriculture is the responsibility of African women, while landownership rights are held by men. Under the terms of customary marriage agreements, a man "buys" the labor of his bride and the couple's future offspring from her family. A woman's economic and social standing rises with the number of children she bears, particularly since children represent extra hands to help with farming, marketing, and other tasks. Each additional child affirms a woman's place within her marriage, ensures her access to land, and fulfills her "obligations" to her husband and her own family. But a woman's claim to her children is nonexistent: In the case of a divorce, mothers generally must leave their children behind.[73]

Such attitudes toward familial relationships dim the prospects of reducing fertility rates in African societies until the status of women improves. Prices paid for brides in expectation of high fertility increase the wealth of a woman's family. Odile Frank and Geoffrey McNicoll, authors of a study on population policy in Kenya, note that, because men bear little financial or domestic reponsibility for basic subsistence, the costs of large numbers of children are invisible to them. As a result, they write, "Even an emerging land shortage is not

> "Until female education is widespread; until women gain at least partial control over their economic lives, high fertility, poverty, and environmental degradation will persist in many regions of the world."

necessarily felt by men as a reason to limit fertility." Policies aimed at capping and regulating bride-price payments as well as those recognizing and enforcing a woman's right to lay claim to land may serve to at least partially counteract the social forces that underlie high levels of fertility.[74]

Improving the status of women—more specifically, reducing their economic dependence on men—is a crucial aspect of development. Until female education is widespread; until women gain at least partial control over the resources that shape their economic lives, high fertility, poverty, and environmental degradation will persist in many regions of the world.

## Filling the Gap

Policymakers concerned with population dynamics are faced with two objectives: reducing the unmet need for family planning in intermediate fertility countries and, in high fertility countries, creating an environment in which small families can become the norm. Helping couples achieve that norm will require a major commitment to family planning from both the international community and Third World nations. But uncertain economic prospects, competing investment needs, and international politics have subverted the growing support for family planning in developing countries. Without the resources needed to back that commitment, the trend of declining fertility may be reversed.

Over the past two decades, about $10 billion has been spent on family planning programs in developing countries, with $4 billion coming from donor countries and the rest from developing countries themselves. The current budget from public and private sources for family planning and population activities in developing countries is about $2.5 billion per year. Donor countries have spent about $500 million per year in this area. The Chinese government alone spends about $1 billion, while the Indian government spends roughly $530 million.[75]

The international community, particularly the United States, has traditionally played a significant role in international family planning.

Recently, however, the United States—the largest dollar contributor in absolute terms—has scaled back its commitment to international population assistance. U.S. funding fell 20 percent between 1985 and 1987, from $288 million to $230 million.[76]

More significantly, the United States no longer contributes to the United Nations Fund for Population Activities (UNFPA) or the International Planned Parenthood Federation. At the International Conference on Population in Mexico City, the Reagan administration set in motion a policy denying funds to any international organization that alerted women to abortion as one of their options. UNFPA funds were withdrawn as a result of U.S. opposition to grants it made to China for census-taking. More than 340 million couples in 65 countries are affected by this short-sighted policy.[77]

Instead of cutting back on international family planning assistance, the United States and other industrial countries need to increase their contributions. Dr. Joseph Speidel of the Population Crisis Committee in Washington, D.C., estimates that in order to achieve population stabilization by the end of next century, global expenditures must rise to $7 billion annually. Industrial countries could contribute at least $2 billion of this total.[78]

An increase in international donor assistance can be used to strengthen family planning in several key areas. First, improving the statistics-gathering and analytical capabilities of Third World governments is essential to charting and responding to trends more accurately. The World Fertility Survey completed in 1984 should be seen as a starting point for ongoing surveys of reproductive health, changing family size, and contraceptive needs. More and better data is needed if developing countries are to build effective programs.

Second, priority should be given to building effective programs in the poorest, most rapidly growing countries, such as those in sub-Saharan Africa and parts of Asia, where services are scant but sorely needed. Third, donors can augment funding for programs in countries where current efforts are inadequate. And new approaches to family planning and social change in these countries deserve more support. India and Mexico, for example, are both using the popular media to spread information and promote the concept of smaller families.

Developing countries themselves need to make a greater commitment to family planning, including programs that are adapted to changing circumstances and to cultural requirements. The following steps can be taken by governments to speed fertility declines in the Third World:

Increase the amount of government funds to family planning and primary health care. Developing countries spend more than four times as much on weaponry and upkeep of military forces as they do on overall health (including primary health care and family planning), $150 billion as opposed to $38 billion. The overpopulation, hunger, and political unrest that are likely to result from continued high fertility pose far greater threats to national security than any outside aggressor.[79]

Make family planning and primary health care more accessible. Contraceptive supplies, educational materials, prenatal health care, and information on family health are desperately needed in rural areas throughout the developing world. New approaches to contraceptive marketing and distribution, such as those that rely on local residents and shopkeepers to disseminate information and supplies, are now being tried in a number of countries.

Encourage smaller families through an integrated development strategy. The primary goals of a family planning program are to reduce unmet need for fertility control, to improve maternal and child health through birthspacing, and to eliminate the need for illegal abortion. But combining such efforts with income generation for women, reforestation efforts, small-scale agricultural projects, and improvements in water supply and sanitation will simultaneously reduce births and improve the quality of life.

Adapt programs to local conditions. Although national leadership is needed, encouraging the development of regional, district, and village programs responsive to local needs is essential. Programs patterned after the Thai loan experiment, relying on the input and assistance of village leaders to introduce new ideas, may be the most successful.

Enlist the aid of the private sector. Initiatives in Africa and elsewhere have shown that it is cost-effective for employers to offer primary health care and family planning services which result in better overall health and higher productivity. In Kenya, a group of 50 companies and plantations is the second largest provider of family planning methods. Likewise, in Nigeria, Gulf Oil and Leder Brothers Co. are planning to introduce such programs.[80]

Build a consortium of developing countries to share experiences and expand technological capabilities. Two decades of international family planning experience hold important lessons for designing effective programs and for creating a social environment receptive to smaller families. Countries such as China, India, Mexico, and Thailand can serve as models for different approaches. Sub-Saharan African countries may find that region-wide cooperation on family planning, in the form of training and outreach programs, will strengthen the efforts of individual countries.

As the interdependence of nations becomes increasingly clear, so too does the knowledge that the fate of even the richest nation is intertwined with that of the most destitute. Planning families to reduce births, improve health, and raise living standards is a universal responsibility. No nation should exempt itself from this global effort.

## Notes

**1.** Larry Rohter, "Central American Plight is People in Abundance," *New York Times*, September 6, 1987.

**2.** Population increase based on Population Reference Bureau (PRB), *1987 World Population Data Sheet* (Washington, D.C.: 1987).

**3.** Population Crisis Committee, "Access to Birth Control: A World Assessment," Briefing Paper No. 19, Washington, D.C., October 1987.

**4.** PRB, *1987 World Population Data Sheet;* World Bank, *World Development Report 1986* (New York: Oxford University Press, 1986).

**5.** PRB, *1987 World Population Data Sheet*.

**6.** Anrudh K. Jain, "The Impact of Development and Population Policies on Fertility in India," *Studies in Family Planning*, July/August 1985; PRB, *1987 World Population Data Sheet*; Carl Haub, demographer, Population Reference Bureau, private communication, October 30, 1987.

**7.** PRB, *1987 World Population Data Sheet*.

**8.** Sheila Rule, "African Rift: Birth Control vs. Tradition," *The New York Times*, August 11, 1985.

**9.** United Nations, Department of International Economic and Social Affairs, *Fertility Behavior in the Context of Development: Evidence from the World Fertility Survey* (New York: 1987).

**10.** Indonesia's per capita income from PRB, *1987 World Population Data Sheet;* Kim Streatfield and Ann Larson, "The 1985 Intercensal Survey of Indonesia: Trends in Contraceptive Prevalence," Research Note from the International Population Dynamics Program, The Australian National University, Canberra, Australia, 1987.

**11.** Ronald Freedman, "The Contribution of Social Science Research to Population Policy and Family Planning Program Effectiveness," *Studies in Family Planning*, March/April 1987.

**12.** Samuel H. Preston, "Population Growth and Economic Development," *Environment*, March 1986.

**13.** Ruhul Amin et al., "Family Planning in Bangladesh, 1969 to 1983," *International Family Planning Perspectives*, March 1987.

**14.** Michael A. Koenig et al., "Trends in Family Size Preferences and Contraceptive Use in Matlab, Bangladesh," *Studies in Family Planning*, May/June 1987.

**15.** "Nigeria: 95 Percent of Married Women Want More Children; Contraceptive Use Limited to Abstinence," *International Family Planning Perspectives*,

September 1985; Ann A. Way, Anne R. Cross, and Sushil Kumar, "Family Planning in Botswana, Kenya, and Zimbabwe," *International Family Planning Perspectives*, March 1987.

**16.** Elizabeth S. Maguire, "Population Policy and Program Initiatives in sub-Saharan Africa," paper presented on behalf of the U.S. Agency for International Development to the Congressional Coalition for Population and Development, Washington, D.C., October 29, 1987.

**17.** Esther Boohene and Thomas E. Dow, Jr., "Contraceptive Prevalence and Family Planning Effort in Zimbabwe," *International Family Planning Perspectives*, March 1987.

**18.** Howard I. Goldberg, Fara G. M'Bodji, and Jay S. Friedman, "Fertility and Family Planning in One Region of Senegal," *International Family Planning Perspectives*, December 1986.

**19.** D. L. Nortman, J. Halva, and A. Rabago, "A Cost Benefit Analysis of the Family Planning Program of the Mexican Social Security Administration," paper presented at the general conference of the International Union for the Scientific Study of Population, Florence, Italy, June 5-12, 1985.

**20.** Dennis N.W. Chao and Karen B. Allen, "A Cost Benefit Analysis of Thailand's Family Planning Program," *International Family Planning Perspectives*, September 1984.

**21.** Judith A. Fortney, "The Importance of Family Planning in Reducing Maternal Mortality," *Studies in Family Planning*, March/April 1987; J. Ties Boerma, "Levels of Maternal Mortality in Developing Countries," *Studies in Family Planning*, July/August 1987; Allan Rosenfield and Deborah Maine, "Maternal Mortality—A Neglected Tragedy: Where is the M in MCH?" *The Lancet*, July 13, 1985.

**22.** Beverly Winikoff and Maureen Sullivan, "Assessing the Role of Family Planning in Reducing Maternal Mortality," *Studies in Family Planning*, May/June 1987.

**23.** Fred T. Sai, "Family planning and maternal health care: a common goal," *World Health Forum*, Vol. 7, 1986; Fortney, "The Importance of Family Planning in Reducing Maternal Mortality."

**24.** Christopher Tietze and Stanley K. Henshaw, *Induced Abortion: A World Review 1986* (New York: Alan Guttmacher Institute, 1986); Stanley K. Henshaw, Senior Researcher, Alan Guttmacher Institute, New York, private communication, October 23, 1987; Joseph Speidel, president, Population Crisis Committee, Washington, D.C., private communication, October and November, 1987.

**25.** Worldwatch Institute estimate based on Tietze and Henshaw, *Induced Abortion*; and PRB, *1987 World Population Data Sheet*.

**26.** Winikoff and Sullivan, "Assessing the Role of Family Planning."

**27.** Sai, "Family planning and maternal health care: a common goal"; Fortney, "The Importance of Family Planning in Reducing Maternal Mortality"; Population Information Program, Johns Hopkins University, "Healthier Mothers and Children through Family Planning," Population Reports, Series J, No. 27, Baltimore, Md., May/June 1984.

**28.** Sai, "Family planning and maternal health care: a common goal."

**29.** Ibid.

**30.** Winikoff and Sullivan, "Assessing the Role of Family Planning."

**31.** Ibid.

**32.** Ibid; Rosenfield and Maine, "Maternal Mortality."

**33.** Sai, "Family planning and maternal health care: a common goal." For information on infant mortality and family planning, see James Trussell and Anne R. Pebley, "The Potential Impact of Changes in Fertility on Infant, Child, and Maternal Mortality." *Studies in Family Planning*, November/December 1984.

**34.** World Health Organization, Special Programme on AIDS, "AIDS and Poverty in the Developing World," Policy Focus No. 7, Geneva, Switzerland, 1987.

**35.** Ibid.; Dr. Jeffrey Harris, AIDS Coordinator, U.S. Agency for International Development, Washington, D.C., private communication, October 29, 1987.

**36.** Population Crisis Committee, "Access to Birth Control."

**37.** Dr. Jeffrey Harris, private communication.

**38.** Population Information Program, Johns Hopkins University, "Hormonal Contraception: New LongActing Methods," Population Reports, Series K, No. 3, Baltimore, Md., March/April 1987.

**39.** Ibid.

**40.** Number of users of family planning from Joseph Speidel, Population Crisis Committee, private communication; discussion of natural family planning techniques can be found in Population Crisis Committee, *Natural Family Planning: Periodic Abstinence as a Method of Fertility Control* (Washington, D.C.: 1981).

41. Tietze and Henshaw, *Induced Abortion*.

42. Ibid.

43. Christine A. Bachrach and William D. Mosher, *Use of Contraception in the United States, 1982* (Washington, D.C.: U.S. Department of Health and Human Services, 1984); Linda Atkinson et al., "Prospects for Improved Contraception," *Family Planning Perspectives*, July/August 1980.

44. Atkinson et al., "Prospects for Improved Contraception."

45. Population Information Program, "Hormonal Contraception."

46. Population Crisis Committee, "Issues in Contraceptive Development," Briefing Paper #15, Washington, D.C., May 1985.

47. Population Information Program, "Hormonal Contraception."

48. Ibid; Sandra Woldman, Director of Public Information, Population Council, New York, private communication, November 9, 1987.

49. Atkinson et al., "Prospects for Improved Contraception."

50. Population Information Program, "Hormonal Contraception."

51. Linda Atkinson, Richard Lincoln, and Jacqueline Darroch Forrest, "Worldwide Trends in Funding for Contraceptive Research and Evaluation," *Family Planning Perspectives*, September/October 1985; and Atkinson, Lincoln, and Forrest, "The Next Contraceptive Revolution," *International Family Planning Perspectives*, December 1985.

52. Ibid.

53. Jane E. Hutchings et al., "The IUD After 20 Years: A Review of Worldwide Experience," *International Family Planning Perspectives*, September 1985.

54. Jeanette H. Johnson and Julie Reich, "The New Politics of Natural Family Planning," *International Family Planning Perspectives*, December 1986.

55. Contraceptive prevalence needed to achieve population stabilization from Dr. Joseph Speidel, Population Crisis Committee, private communication.

56. Nancy I. Heckel, "Population Laws and Policies in Sub-Saharan Africa: 1975-1985," *International Family Planning Perspectives*, December 1986.

57. Ibid.; Kenyan official quoted in Rule, "African Rift."

58. Rule, "African Rift."

59. Freedman, "The Contribution of Social Science Research to Population Policy"; John Davies, S.N. Mitra, and William P. Schellstede, "Oral Contracep-

tion in Bangladesh: Social Marketing and the Importance of Husbands," *Studies in Family Planning*, May/June 1987.

60. Freedman, "The Contribution of Social Science Research to Population Policy."

61. Ibid.

62. Population Information Program, Johns Hopkins University, "Population and Birth Planning in the People's Republic of China," Population Reports, Series J, No. 25, Baltimore, Md., January/February 1982. See also Chen Muhua, "Birth Planning in China," *International Family Planning Perspectives*, September 1979; Elisabeth J. Croll, "Production vs. Reproduction: A Threat to China's Development Strategy," *World Development*, Vol. 11, No. 6, 1983; Nathan Keyfitz, "The Population of China," *Scientific American*, February 1984; Arthur P. Wolf, "The Preeminent Role of Government Intervention in China's Family Revolution," *Population and Development Review*, March 1986.

63. Population Information Program, "Population Planning in the People's Republic of China."

64. Ibid.; Nicholas D. Kristof, "China's Birth Rate on Rise Again as Official Sanctions Are Ignored," *The New York Times*, April 21, 1987; Daniel Southerland, "Despite Years of Controls, China Fears New Baby Boom," *Washington Post*, May 24, 1987.

65. Kristof, "China's Birth Rate on Rise Again"; Southerland, "Despite Years of Controls, China Fears New Baby Boom."

66. Marshall Green, "Is China Easing Up on Birth Control?" *The New York Times*, April 28, 1987.

67. Population Information Program, Johns Hopkins University, "The Impact of Family Planning Programs on Fertility," Population Reports, Series J, No. 29, Baltimore, Md., January/February 1985; Alaka M. Basu, "Family Planning and the Emergency: An Unanticipated Consequence," *Economic and Political Weekly*, March 9, 1985.

68. Donald Weeden et al., "An Incentives Program to Increase Contraceptive Prevalence in Rural Thailand," *International Family Planning Perspectives*, March 1986.

69. Ibid.

70. Phillips Cutright, "The Ingredients of Recent Fertility Decline in Developing Countries," *International Family Planning Perspectives*, December 1983.

71. Anrudh K. Jain and Moni Nag, "Female Primary Education and Fertility Education in India," Population Council, Center for Policy Studies, New York,

September 1985; United Nations, Department of International Economic and Social Affairs, *Education and Fertility: Selected Findings from the World Fertility Survey Data* (New York: 1986); United Nations, Department of International Economic and Social Affairs, *Fertility Behavior in the Context of Development*.

72. William U. Chandler, *Investing in Children* (Washington, D.C.: Worldwatch Institute, 1985).

73. Odile Frank and Geoffrey McNicoll, "An Interpretation of Fertility and Population Policy in Kenya," Center for Policy Studies Working Papers, No. 131, The Population Council, New York, February 1987.

74. Ibid.

75. Joseph Speidel, Population Crisis Committee, private communication.

76. Ibid.

77. Ibid.

78. Ibid.

79. Ruth Leger Sivard, *World Military and Social Expenditures 1986* (Washington, D.C.: World Priorities, 1986).

80. Elizabeth Maguire, Chief of the Population Policy Division, U.S. Agency for International Development, Washington, D.C., private communication, October 29, 1987.

---

**Jodi L. Jacobson** is a Researcher with Worldwatch Institute. She has coauthored Worldwatch papers on demographic and socioeconomic issues, and is a coauthor of *State of the World 1987* and *State of the World 1988*. She is a graduate of the University of Wisconsin-Madison where she studied economics and environmental science.

# THE WORLDWATCH PAPER SERIES

**No. of Copies***

- _____ 1. **The Other Energy Crisis: Firewood** by Erik Eckholm.
- _____ 3. **Women in Politics: A Global Review** by Kathleen Newland.
- _____ 7. **The Unfinished Assignment: Equal Education for Women** by Patricia L. McGrath.
- _____ 10. **Health: The Family Planning Factor** by Erik Eckholm and Kathleen Newland.
- _____ 13. **Spreading Deserts—The Hand of Man** by Erik Eckholm and Lester R. Brown.
- _____ 16. **Women and Population Growth: Choice Beyond Childbearing** by Kathleen Newland.
- _____ 18. **Cutting Tobacco's Toll** by Erik Eckholm.
- _____ 21. **Soft Technologies, Hard Choices** by Colin Norman.
- _____ 25. **Worker Participation—Productivity and the Quality of Work Life** by Bruce Stokes.
- _____ 28. **Global Employment and Economic Justice: The Policy Challenge** by Kathleen Newland.
- _____ 29. **Resource Trends and Population Policy: A Time for Reassessment** by Lester R. Brown.
- _____ 30. **The Dispossessed of the Earth: Land Reform and Sustainable Development** by Erik Eckholm.
- _____ 31. **Knowledge and Power: The Global Research and Development Budget** by Colin Norman.
- _____ 33. **International Migration: The Search for Work** by Kathleen Newland.
- _____ 34. **Inflation: The Rising Cost of Living on a Small Planet** by Robert Fuller.
- _____ 35. **Food or Fuel: New Competition for the World's Cropland** by Lester R. Brown.
- _____ 36. **The Future of Synthetic Materials: The Petroleum Connection** by Christopher Flavin.
- _____ 37. **Women, Men, and The Division of Labor** by Kathleen Newland.
- _____ 38. **City Limits: Emerging Constraints on Urban Growth** by Kathleen Newland.
- _____ 39. **Microelectronics at Work: Productivity and Jobs in the World Economy** by Colin Norman.
- _____ 40. **Energy and Architecture: The Solar and Conservation Potential** by Christopher Flavin.
- _____ 41. **Men and Family Planning** by Bruce Stokes.
- _____ 42. **Wood: An Ancient Fuel with a New Future** by Nigel Smith.
- _____ 43. **Refugees: The New International Politics of Displacement** by Kathleen Newland.
- _____ 44. **Rivers of Energy: The Hydropower Potential** by Daniel Deudney.
- _____ 45. **Wind Power: A Turning Point** by Christopher Flavin.
- _____ 46. **Global Housing Prospects: The Resource Constraints** by Bruce Stokes.
- _____ 47. **Infant Mortality and the Health of Societies** by Kathleen Newland.
- _____ 48. **Six Steps to a Sustainable Society** by Lester R. Brown and Pamela Shaw.
- _____ 49. **Productivity: The New Economic Context** by Kathleen Newland.
- _____ 50. **Space: The High Frontier in Perspective** by Daniel Deudney.
- _____ 51. **U.S. and Soviet Agriculture: The Shifting Balance of Power** by Lester R. Brown.
- _____ 52. **Electricity from Sunlight: The Future of Photovoltaics** by Christopher Flavin.

*Worldwatch Papers 2, 4, 5, 6, 8, 9, 11, 12, 14, 15, 17, 19, 20, 22, 23, 24, 26, 27, and 32 are out of print.

_____ 53. **Population Policies for a New Economic Era** by Lester R. Brown.
_____ 54. **Promoting Population Stabilization** by Judith Jacobsen.
_____ 55. **Whole Earth Security: A Geopolitics of Peace** by Daniel Deudney.
_____ 56. **Materials Recycling: The Virtue of Necessity** by William U. Chandler.
_____ 57. **Nuclear Power: The Market Test** by Christopher Flavin.
_____ 58. **Air Pollution, Acid Rain, and the Future of Forests** by Sandra Postel.
_____ 59. **Improving World Health: A Least Cost Strategy** by William U. Chandler.
_____ 60. **Soil Erosion: Quiet Crisis in the World Economy** by Lester Brown and Edward Wolf.
_____ 61. **Electricity's Future: The Shift to Efficiency and Small-Scale Power** by Christopher Flavin.
_____ 62. **Water: Rethinking Management in an Age of Scarcity** by Sandra Postel.
_____ 63. **Energy Productivity: Key to Environmental Protection and Economic Progress** by William U. Chandler.
_____ 64. **Investing in Children** by William U. Chandler.
_____ 65. **Reversing Africa's Decline** by Lester Brown and Edward Wolf.
_____ 66. **World Oil: Coping With the Dangers of Success** by Christopher Flavin.
_____ 67. **Conserving Water: The Untapped Alternative** by Sandra Postel.
_____ 68. **Banishing Tobacco** by William U. Chandler.
_____ 69. **Decommissioning: Nuclear Power's Missing Link** by Cynthia Pollock.
_____ 70. **Electricity For A Developing World** by Christopher Flavin.
_____ 71. **Altering the Earth's Chemistry: Assessing the Risks** by Sandra Postel.
_____ 72. **The Changing Role of the Market in National Economies** by William U. Chandler.
_____ 73. **Beyond the Green Revolution: New Approaches for Third World Agriculture** by Edward C. Wolf.
_____ 74. **Our Demographically Divided World** by Lester R. Brown and Jodi L. Jacobson.
_____ 75. **Reassessing Nuclear Power: The Fallout From Chernobyl** by Christopher Flavin.
_____ 76. **Mining Urban Wastes: The Potential for Recycling** by Cynthia Pollock.
_____ 77. **The Future of Urbanization: Facing the Ecological and Economic Constraints** by Lester R. Brown and Jodi L. Jacobson.
_____ 78. **On the Brink of Extinction: Conserving Biological Diversity** by Edward C. Wolf.
_____ 79. **Defusing the Toxics Threat: Controlling Pesticides and Industrial Waste** by Sandra Postel.
_____ 80. **Planning the Global Family** by Jodi L. Jacobson

_____ **Total Copies**

**Bulk Copies** (any combination of titles)　　　　　　　　**Single Copy**　$4.00
　　2-5: $3.00 each　6-20: $2.00 each　21 or more: $1.00 each

**Calendar Year Subscription** (1988 subscription begins with Paper 81)　U.S. $25.00 _____

**Make check payable to Worldwatch Institute**
1776 Massachusetts Avenue NW, Washington, D.C. 20036 USA

　　　　　　　　　　　　　　　　Enclosed is my check for U.S. $ _____

_____
**name**
_____
**address**
_____
**city**　　　　　　　　　　**state**　　　　　　　　　　**zip/country**